DR. FAUCI

A Little Golden Book® Biography

By Suzanne Slade
Illustrated by Fanny Liem

A GOLDEN BOOK • NEW YORK

Educators and librarians, for a variety of teaching tools, visit us at RHTeachersLibrarians.com
Library of Congress Control Number: 2021941335
ISBN 978-0-593-48406-7 (trade) — ISBN 978-0-593-48407-4 (ebook)
Printed in the United States of America
10 9 8 7 6 5 4 3 2 1

Anthony Fauci is a doctor and a scientist who has helped keep America healthy for over fifty years.

Tony, as he is often called, was born in Brooklyn, New York, on Christmas Eve in 1940. He grew up in the Italian American section of Brooklyn because his grandparents had emigrated from Italy years before. The families in Tony's neighborhood were warm and caring.

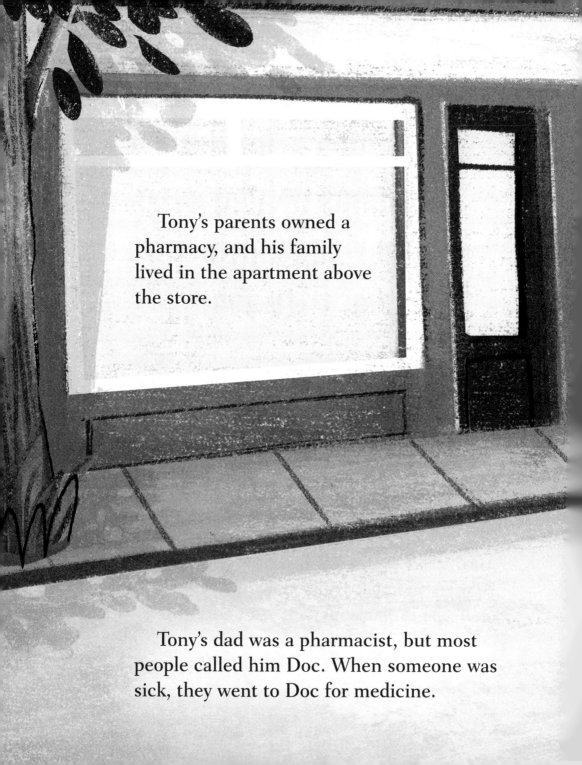

Tony's parents owned a pharmacy, and his family lived in the apartment above the store.

Tony's dad was a pharmacist, but most people called him Doc. When someone was sick, they went to Doc for medicine.

The whole family helped run the store. Tony's mom and older sister worked the cash register. Tony rode his bicycle around town delivering orders. He liked helping people get better.

The Fauci family attended the Catholic church across the street from their pharmacy. After Mass, Tony enjoyed sharing huge meals of meatballs and pasta with his aunts, uncles, and cousins.

Tony and his buddies loved talking about baseball. They often argued about which players and which team were the best. His friends rooted for the Brooklyn Dodgers, but Tony was a New York Yankees fan. One of his favorite players was Joe DiMaggio, a powerful hitter who could send the ball soaring!

In 1954, Tony started attending Regis High School, a free Catholic boys' school that attracted New York's top students. He had to ride subways and buses for over an hour to get from his home in Brooklyn to school on the Upper East Side of Manhattan.

Tony excelled in his classes and was captain of the basketball team. A fast player and a great shooter, he hoped to play professional ball someday, but he never grew taller than five foot seven. So Tony began thinking about other careers.

Tony was fascinated by his high school science classes, and he loved being with people. He considered jobs that included both. Eventually, he knew what he wanted to be— a doctor! Tony took premed classes in college to prepare for medical school.

Each summer, Tony worked on a construction crew. One year, he helped build a library at Cornell Medical College. During a lunch break, he sneaked into the school's auditorium. As he walked through the door, the thought of attending this great school gave him goose bumps.

A guard told him to leave. Tony explained his dream of one day attending Cornell and becoming a doctor. The guard laughed. But Tony was determined. The next year, he was accepted at Cornell Medical College. And in 1966, he graduated first in his class!

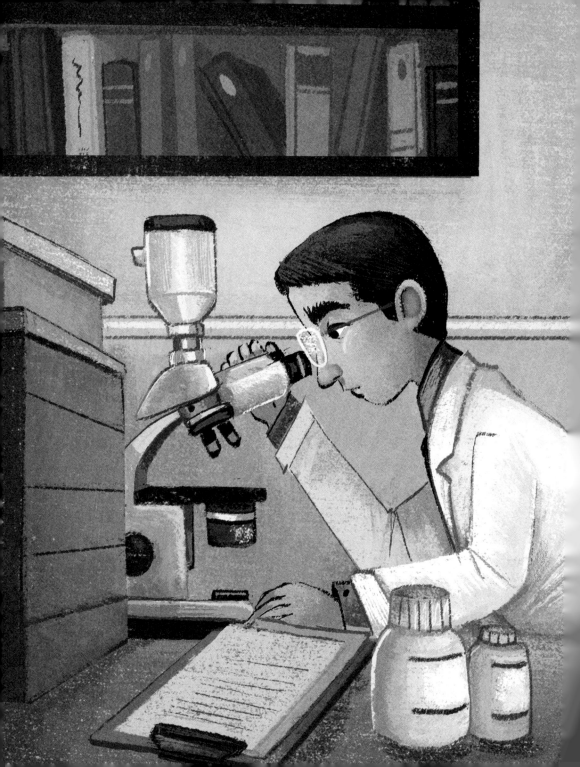

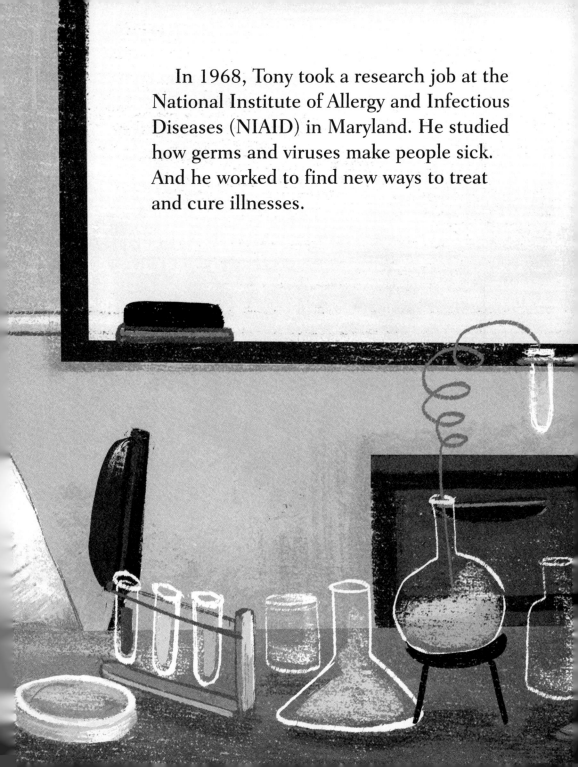

In 1968, Tony took a research job at the National Institute of Allergy and Infectious Diseases (NIAID) in Maryland. He studied how germs and viruses make people sick. And he worked to find new ways to treat and cure illnesses.

Tony also treated patients in hospitals. At one hospital, he met a nurse named Christine. She was smart, kind, and beautiful. Tony invited her to dinner. They fell in love and married a year later. In time, they had three little girls.

Tony's job kept him busy. He worked fourteen hours a day, as well as on weekends. His family waited until he got home at nine p.m. to eat dinner together. And after his daughters went to sleep, Tony worked more.

In the 1980s, Tony focused his research on a disease called AIDS, which is caused by a virus named HIV.

AIDS soon spread around the world, and many people died. Tony searched for medicines to fight HIV. Some patients grew angry because testing and approving the medicines took so long. Tony listened to their ideas, and they began to work together. He helped scientists find medicines that gave AIDS patients much longer, healthier lives. In 2008, President George W. Bush awarded Tony the Presidential Medal of Freedom for his work in fighting AIDS.

Year after year, Tony kept up his busy schedule. He developed successful treatments for serious diseases that had stumped other doctors.

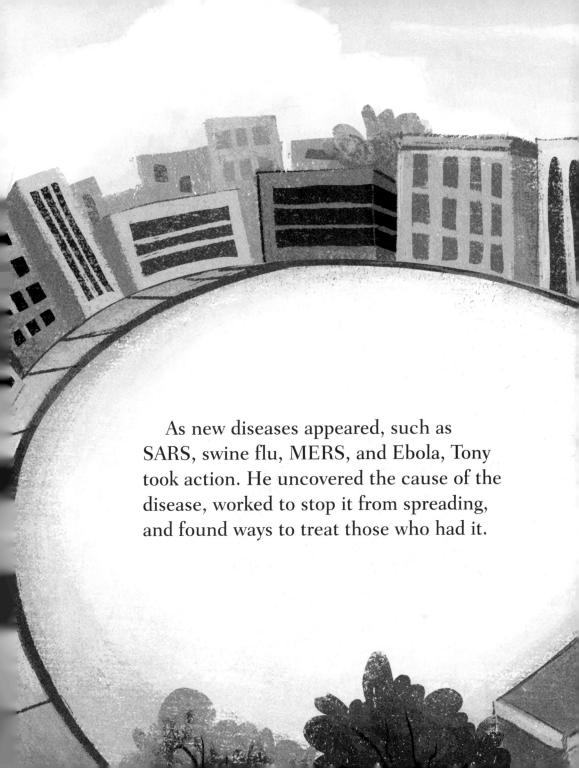

As new diseases appeared, such as SARS, swine flu, MERS, and Ebola, Tony took action. He uncovered the cause of the disease, worked to stop it from spreading, and found ways to treat those who had it.

In December 2019, some people in China got an illness named COVID-19. It was caused by something called a coronavirus. This disease could easily spread from one person to another.

Soon, people in many countries got COVID-19. The world was surprised by the growing pandemic, but Tony wasn't. He had been battling new viruses for decades.

The mysterious illness scared people, and Tony calmly shared scientific facts about COVID-19 in a way that everyone could understand. He explained how people could protect themselves. Thanks to Tony, they began to feel less frightened.

Tony knew that scientists and the public needed to work together to slow the spread of COVID-19. He asked everyone to stay home more, keep a safe distance from others, wear masks over their nose and mouth, and wash their hands. He told people to avoid crowded places, like restaurants and theaters.

Researchers began developing vaccines to protect people from COVID-19. Tony made sure the vaccines were carefully tested on thousands of volunteers.

In December 2020, scientists declared great news: the vaccines were safe and effective! People around the world lined up to get their shots.

COVID-19 vaccination center

Dr. Fauci has spent his life helping others. As "America's doctor," Tony has worked with seven U.S. presidents. And through the years, whenever a new health crisis has come up, each president has relied on Dr. Fauci's expert advice.

The world is a healthier place because of Dr. Anthony Fauci!